Cowboy Slim's Dude Ranch

by Gary Miller

illustrated by John Kurtz

Scott Foresman
is an imprint of

Glenview, Illinois • Boston, Massachusetts • Chandler, Arizona
Upper Saddle River, New Jersey

Illustrator CVR, 3-15 John Kurtz

Photographs
Every effort has been made to secure permission and provide appropriate credit for photographic material. The publisher deeply regrets any omission and pledges to correct errors called to its attention in subsequent editions.

Unless otherwise acknowledged, all photographs are the property of Pearson Education, Inc.

16 © Horace Bristol/Corbis

ISBN 13: 978-0-328-51414-4
ISBN 10:   0-328-51414-4

9 10 V0FL 16 15 14

It was a typical, quiet Friday night at the Williams home. That is, until Dad came home from work with a big, goofy smile on his face. But it wasn't the smile that puzzled Danny; it was the way Dad was dressed. He had a red cotton handkerchief tied around his neck, and he wore a giant white cowboy hat.

Danny gave Dad a curious look, but Dad just kept smiling.

"Dad, why are you dressed like that?" Danny asked.

"I'm not telling. It's your job to guess," said Dad.

Before Danny could make his first guess, Mom walked in the room.

"Mom, why is Dad dressed like that?" Danny asked.

Mom just smiled. Without saying a word, she stepped into the other room. When she returned, she, too, was wearing a cowboy hat and a handkerchief.

"Okay, try to guess," urged Mom.

Danny thought Mom and Dad both looked completely ridiculous, but he was ready to make his guess.

"I think you must be going to some kind of a costume party," Danny said. "Maybe a cowboy festival?"

"No, but we *are* going somewhere," said Dad, "and you're going too."

Then Dad took a piece of paper out of his briefcase. It was a flyer for Cowboy Slim's Dude Ranch.

Danny had never heard of a dude ranch, so Mom and Dad explained.

"A dude ranch is a real, live, working ranch where people can go for a vacation," Dad said.

"While we're there, we'll ride horses, do chores, and eat grub," said Mom. "We'll even dress like cowhands."

Danny couldn't believe what he was hearing. He lived in the suburbs of Chicago and had always wanted to visit the West. He had always wanted to ride a horse and sleep outside at night under the pale light of the stars. As far as Danny was concerned, there was only one problem with going to a dude ranch.

"That sounds great, but there is *no way* I am going to dress up in those silly clothes," Danny said.

The next morning, Danny and his parents packed for their dude ranch vacation. Danny packed his blue jeans, tee shirts, sneakers, socks, and underwear. He packed his camera too. But there was one thing he didn't want to pack.

Mom and Dad wanted to bring Danny's cowboy clothes for their stay at the ranch, and Danny hated them. But Mom insisted on bringing the clothes along—just in case Danny changed his mind.

A few days later, Danny and his parents set out and drove west for a long time. They crossed three states to get to Colorado! Finally they arrived in ranch country. Cattle stood by the side of the long, flat road, and Danny even saw a few cowhands herding cattle in the distance.

When they arrived at Cowboy Slim's Dude Ranch, Danny was amazed. "Wow, this is incredible!" he said. The dude ranch looked just like ranches he had seen in the movies.

A moment later a tall cowboy came out to greet Danny's family and the other new arrivals with smiles and handshakes. It was Cowboy Slim from the brochure! He was slim, but muscular from years of riding horses and working on the ranch. His tan skin was weathered from the sun and wind. Danny admired the way he wore his leather boots and wide hat. For some reason, the clothes didn't look silly on Cowboy Slim.

Before Slim finished welcoming his guests to the ranch, Danny had already decided he wanted to be just like Slim.

The next morning, everyone ate breakfast in the ranch house. Then it was time for chores. To feed the horses, Danny had to throw hay bales down from the loft. His hands got red and sore.

"If you wear your gloves, your hands won't get scraped," said Slim.

Danny went back to the bunkhouse and got his gloves. Slim was right—they worked perfectly.

These gloves don't look so silly on me after all, Danny thought to himself.

That afternoon, Danny and his parents went out to help repair some fences. The sun was hot, and sweat ran into Danny's eyes.

"You should wear a hat like mine," said Slim. "It shades your face from the sun. And carry a handkerchief so you can use it to wipe the sweat from your face."

Danny went back to the bunkhouse to get his hat and handkerchief.

"There's a reason why cowhands wear these," Danny told Dad. "And they actually look kind of cool."

Soon the sun got even hotter, and Danny noticed that his arms were getting sunburned.

"What should I do?" he asked Slim.

"Go put on a long-sleeved shirt. Cotton shirts help keep you cool, and the sleeves protect your arms from the sun."

Danny went back to the bunkhouse. He put on his new shirt. He looked in the mirror.

"I'm starting to look like a real cowboy," he said to himself.

That afternoon, Slim saddled some horses. The chores were finished, and now it was time for some fun.

"We're going riding," Slim said, "so you need to put on your chaps and boots."

This time, Danny didn't think twice. He put on his leather chaps and his black cowboy boots. He tried walking a few paces. The boots felt snug and comfortable. Now Danny was ready to ride a horse.

Soon everyone was riding across the plains. Slim led the way on his graceful chestnut mare.

Danny and his parents followed behind. At first Danny felt clumsy, then he began to feel the rhythm of the horse's movement. Before long, he was riding like he'd been doing it for years.

The landscape was rugged, but Danny's new clothes helped out. The boots kept Danny's feet in the stirrups. The chaps protected Danny's legs from brush and thorns.

Danny felt like a real cowhand! He'd never been happier.

All week long, Danny lived like a cowhand. He rode horses, helped herd cattle, and even learned to rope a steer. When the week was over and it was time to leave, Danny was sad.

"Remember, you're welcome back anytime," Slim said.

That afternoon, Danny began to pack.

"Aren't you going to change back into your regular clothes for the trip home?" Mom asked.

Danny gave Mom a proud look. "No way. I'm a cowboy now," he said. "And I can't wait to show these clothes to my friends!"

A Cattle Drive

In the mid-1700s, ranchers began to raise beef cattle on vast ranches in Texas. By 1850 many ranchers used cattle drives to bring their cattle to markets in the North and West.

In the spring, a group of cowhands on horses rounded up herds of 2,000 or more cattle and drove them to markets or railroad towns.

Cattle drives often covered hundreds of miles. To keep the cattle together, cowhands had to be skilled riders. They had to know how to protect their cattle from wild animals and cattle thieves.

Today, ranchers still raise and sell cattle, but cattle drives are now a thing of the past.